FOUNDATIONS FOR SUCCESS

EIGHT WEEKS TO REAL ESTATE SUCCESS

VOLUME 4
BUYERS, BUYERS, BUYERS

Stephen L. Silver, BScPT

Broker

This publication is designed to provide information with regard to the subject matter covered. It is sold with the understanding that the author and publisher are not engaged in rendering legal, accounting or other professional advice. If legal advice or other expert assistance is required, the services of a competent professional person should be sought.

ISBN 13: 978-0-9939401-5-6

BUYERS, BUYERS, BUYERS

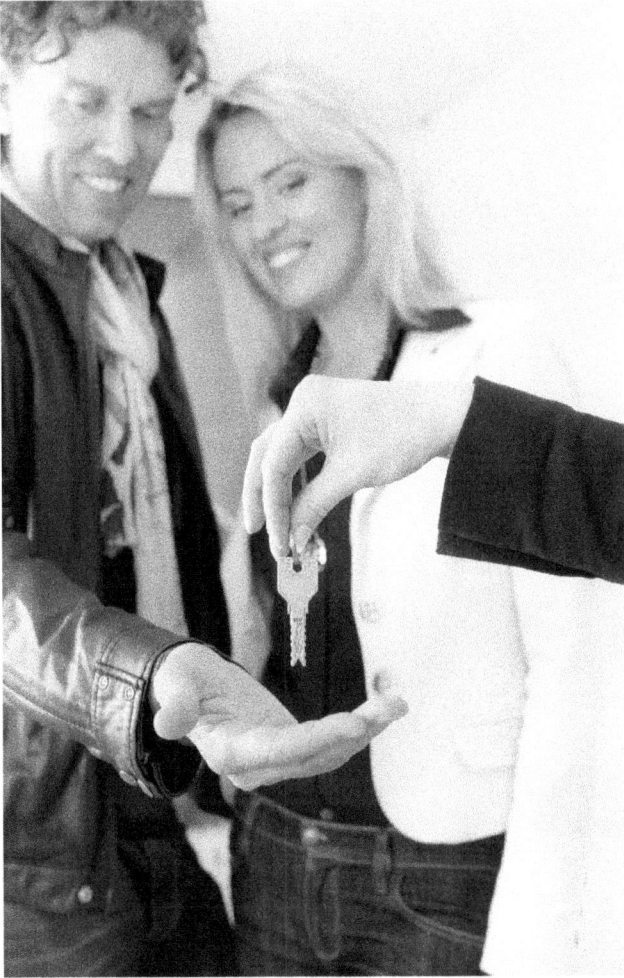

"Owning a home is a keystone of wealth - both financial affluence and emotional security."

Suze Orman

Contents

Foreword

Recently a new Salesperson revealed to me what most newly licensed individuals experience... *"Bruce, when I got my real estate license, it seemed like they gave me the keys to the car but then nobody taught me how to drive it."* There's a lot of wisdom in that analogy and...no doubt a lot of frustration for people starting out.

In his first book, *List to Last*, Stephen Silver focused on prospecting for, closing on and managing listings. In his second book, *Foundations for Success*, Steve takes you through a very detailed process of "how to drive a car." As a new REALTOR®, you need to take time to develop your business without wasting time and money. You'll learn how to:

- Develop a simple business plan that will take you on the trip from where you are now to where you want to be.
- Avoid the most common traps in which new REALTORS® get caught.
- Implement the systems that help you:
  - Become organized, in terms of managing time, finances and clients.
  - Connect with and cultivate the leads you'll need to develop in order to secure a consistent, reproducible business.
  - Manage listings and buyers from start to finish.

This book provides specific business building exercises for you to complete that will utilize the information provided and get you on track to success fast. You'll see how you can achieve the success you deserve and grow your business at a significantly greater rate than you ever thought.

I have known Steve Silver for a long time... he knows the business inside out and is an excellent "driving instructor." Follow these steps, take them on chapter by chapter and you too will be "a great driver". Good luck...turn the key and start your engine!

Bruce Keith

Bruce Keith is a leading Motivational Speaker and Trainer for sales organizations in North America, specializing in Real Estate Sales.

He has been in real estate in excess of 27 years, including 16 years as a top Coach for thousands of Sales Agents. Learn more at www.BruceKeithResults.com.

Acknowledgements

Bruce Keith, mentor, coach and long-time friend, for sharing his experience, his encouragement and recommendations, which made the publishing of this series possible.

Aileen Simcic, my best friend and business partner, for her support and encouragement through the many years of our shared real estate practice and beyond and her husband, Christopher Hairrell, for putting up with it all.

Bohdan Uszkalo, friend, business partner and general wild and crazy guy, who always had a joke (not always great) and an encouraging word.

Gerald Tostowaryk, whose personal and professional life defines the meaning of ethics and character and who kept me pointed in the right direction when I needed it.

Dan Gitzel, friend, Broker and mentor, who gave me the chance to find my way back to what I love, teaching and helping others and without whom none of this would have been possible.

David Yunker, ever present and ever available friend, mentor and sounding board, without whose guidance and advice this work would have oft gone astray.

Virginia Munden whose example of dedication to teaching and mentoring has been an inspiration and for taking the time from her ridiculously busy schedule to help me get this book into a readable condition.

ACKNOWLEDGEMENTS

George Zanette, friend and trusted advisor, whose advice has been instrumental in getting this book into a format that makes sense to more people than just me.

Christina Davie, friend, major support and chief architect of my endurance, without whom I would have either called it quits or be sitting in prison for murder.

Josie Stern, friend, inspiration and SuperREALTOR®, for demonstrating, on a daily basis, that the main thesis of this book, having and consistently using systems as well as an unwavering commitment to client service, are the only ways to succeed in real estate.

And finally, but most importantly, to my family, my father Gerald, and daughters Arielle and Andrea, who endured my neglect, ordered in food, and my mood swings and still gave me their unrelenting support, encouragement and love. Without you, this would never have been possible.

Introduction

Systems for Success

Real estate sales can be a siren song to many. To those outside the business it appears to be an easy way to make money. Watch any of the home improvement channels and you can see people flipping this house, flipping that house, real estate agents selling million dollar properties to the first people that walk in the door, turning junk homes into gorgeous properties and renting them out to the first group through. And all this happens during an hour long show. So many get into the business with the dream of earning a huge income in their first few months, but it's a sad fact of life in the real estate world that almost 50% of new Sales Representatives fail and are out of the business within the first year of graduating from the training programs. And a further 50% of the remaining aspirants drop out within the second year.

This happens for a wide range of reasons, but the most common one is that the initial training programs don't adequately educate them on the realities of life in the real world as a REALTOR®. They're taught how to avoid getting into trouble with the provincial regulators. They're taught the basics of real estate law and they're taught such useful tools as the length of a "chain", metes and bounds or the Torrens system. There's little to no training on what is truly necessary to succeed in this most competitive business, systems.

That's why this series has been written. It's designed to provide new salespeople with the information, tools, skills and systems they'll require to help them get through those first couple of difficult years.

In this series can be found a step by step approach to implementing the systems that every successful real estate salesperson requires, beginning with business planning and time management and moving through organizational systems, prospecting, working with sellers and buyers and much more. Tools and business building exercises are included, both in the series, the workbook and online at www.foundationsforsuccess.ca which will assist the salesperson in developing those systems, their skills and confidence.

Volume 1 – On the Right Foot will introduce you to the Business Plan, the real secret behind getting started without falling into the traps encountered by most new Sales Representatives. It will also introduce you to the key components of success, consistency and organization; doing what needs to be done, when it needs to be done, as often as it needs to be done, in every aspect of the business, including time, client and financial management.

Volume 2 – Good Hunting will familiarize you with various types of prospecting techniques, and even more importantly than the types of techniques, you'll learn to develop the mindset required to be consistently successful at it. You'll be shown how to develop and maintain one of the most important long-term prospecting activities, a farm, an activity which will establish you as the best known and most knowledgeable REALTOR® in the area. We'll review the many different active forms that prospecting may take, including making prospecting calls, door-knocking, Open Houses, converting For Sale By Owners, networking, trade shows, and participating in client and community events.

Volume 2 will examine not just lead generation but will also help you develop a complete and organized lead follow up system, so that the leads you generate result in ongoing and future business. You'll read about how to follow up with leads rapidly, effectively and to set them up on a program that keeps you in touch with them until they're ready to act.

In **Volume 3 – Listings, Listings, Listings** you'll read about, and prepare a listing system that differentiates you from other REALTORS® and helps influence people to want to work with you before they actually meet you. It discusses listing presentations that demonstrate to the potential client that you're able to provide them with the value they're seeking and what they feel is important, not what you believe your value is. You'll also learn to develop a highly organized listing system that ensures you follow a consistent process for every listing, thereby reducing or eliminating the possibility of missing any steps throughout the entire sales cycle.

Volume 3 will also review and discuss offer management, a key component of a well-constructed listing system. The management of offers, both single and multiple, can easily become disorganized and chaotic without a standardized method of handling the many aspects of what can be a complex procedure.

In **Volume 4 – Buyers, Buyers, Buyers** you'll read about different buyer demographics, what the average buyer in each is looking for when purchasing a home and the questions that will help you determine what your client is looking for, what type of buyer they are and that will help you narrow down their needs and wants. By following the systems in this volume, you should be able to review the properties for which they're looking and help you find them the right property in the least amount of time.

As in Volume 3, this volume will help you develop a buyers' system, including an offer management system for your buyer which will enable you to protect your client's interests while obtaining the property with the least amount of difficulty.

And in **Volume 5 – I'm Just Sayin'**, you'll be introduced to a critical skill you'll need to develop, objection handling. Using the BASIQ technique, introduced in this volume, you'll be able to quickly and easily determine what the true objection is and by asking the right questions and listening carefully to the answers you'll have the opportunity to understand what the client's concern is and, even more, how to handle it.

The next critical skill you'll need to cultivate is your communication abilities, in order to eliminate the major source of complaints against REALTORS®, a lack of communication or a miscommunication that was never resolved. This volume will discuss how your ongoing task will be to, through the use of open ended questions and active listening techniques, fully grasp what your client is trying to communicate to you as well as ensuring that the client is able to clearly hear and understand the information you're providing.

You'll also be introduced to negotiation, which, if not prepared for, can be a very disconcerting experience. You'll learn how to work towards a win-win resolution, how to prepare for the negotiation and how to develop and execute an effective game plan, complete with specific strategies to achieve the desired outcomes.

And last, this volume will provide you with direction on marketing and advertising. As with any other system, your marketing strategy must planned out for the year so that you don't miss any component or spend money where you needn't, a major point of failure for most new salespeople. You'll learn how to write ads that appeal to buyers.

And finally **Volume 6 – The Workbook** will provide you with a weekly, step by step approach to building and managing your business. You'll have opportunities to develop, in a logical, proven, sequence by completing the exercises provided, the systems, skills, and tools you'll need to smooth out the learning curve, reduce the time required to implement the systems needed to ensure their success and begin earning a steady, reproducible and predictable income in a shorter period of time.

However, it is not the end of what you need to do and what you need to learn. As with any athlete, learning the rudiments of the sport is just the beginning. Stop learning and perfecting your skills and techniques and you end up being nothing more than average at best. Professional and high caliber amateur athletes all recognize that the key to ongoing success is to have someone who can teach them and hold them accountable for their performance, forcing them to take absolute advantage of their strengths as well as to face their weaknesses and overcome them; in other words, a coach. I strongly urge you to consider working with a real estate coach who can help you hone your skills and techniques, provide you with additional tools and skills designed to test your limits, push you to excel and ensure you reach the goals you'll set for yourself.

CHAPTER 1

Buyers, Buyers, Buyers

In the previous volume we examined how to find and work with listings. As a new Sales Representative, it's very likely that your first few deals will come from working with buyers. In this volume we're going to take a look at how best to service those clients. Before beginning to discuss the Buyers' System, it's important to understand where buyers come from, why they buy and why, as a new Sales Representative, it's important to work with them.

The 2014 National Association of REALTORS (NAR) Generational Trends Report found that Millennials (people aged 22 – 35) made up the largest share of home buyers at 31 percent, 76% of whom were first time buyers, followed by people aged 35 - 50 (Gen X) and the Baby Boomers each at 30 percent. Seniors only accounted for approximately 9 percent of total buyers.

"About half of millennial buyers primarily purchased a home just for the desire to own a home of their own. Gen X placed a high importance on owning a home of their own, but many needed a larger home and needed to move for a job-related relocation. Older Boomers and the Silent Generation are more likely to move for retirement, the desire to be closer to friends, family, and relatives, and the desire for a smaller home."

Millennial buyers place a high priority on convenience to both their job and lifestyle options as well as the affordability of the homes they're viewing. They also try to stay close, usually within

7

10 miles, to their previous residence, while older generations tend to move longer distances, typically up to 30 miles from their previous home. Boomers and seniors place a higher priority on convenience to friends and family, convenience to shopping, and convenience to health facilities.

Younger buyers tend to be willing to compromise on many factors in the home they purchase, such as the price of the home, distance from job, size of the home, and condition of the home purchased. However, the older generations are usually less willing to compromise on the features of the homes they purchase, as they want to avoid the additional costs and headaches associated with renovating.

When looking for a home, it's no surprise that all generations begin their search process by looking online; however, Millennials tend to spend more time online researching the homes, communities and the REALTOR® before making contact. Older buyers are more likely to be more occasional users during their home search and tend to contact a REALTOR® once they've done some research.

An interesting factor that became clear in the NAR study was that the search time for a home was different for the various age groups, with older buyers tending to take a shorter period of time to find their next home than younger buyers. The study demonstrated that younger buyers (under age 59) tend to search for a home for 12 weeks. Buyer aged between 59 and 67 tend to look for 10 weeks and older buyers (68 to 88 years of age) search for just 8 weeks.

Why work with buyers?

I know, everyone, including me, says that in this business, you need to list to last. You have to focus on getting listings. And I firmly believe that. However, you're more than likely going to find that, for the first year or two, you'll work with more buyers than sellers. And that's OK, because working with buyers gives you many different opportunities to develop critical success factors that will stand you in good stead in the future, not to mention an income.

You'll get the chance to develop and hone skills, such as prospecting and objection handling, asking the right questions and active listening, recognizing and adapting your client handling skills to different personality types, writing and negotiating offers and many more. You'll develop time management and prioritization skills.

And even more importantly, you'll have the chance to develop your reputation, both with clients and with your colleagues. You'll learn how to build and maintain trust with your clients and how to avoid the many traps which can create roadblocks to that trust and reputation.

What's your role?

A good buyer's agent is able to carry out a series of essential tasks that reach far beyond just searching for properties. They must:

- Know how to ask the questions needed to uncover the buyer's needs and wants as well as their major motivating factor in the purchase.

- Become a trusted adviser and supporter during the entire home buying process.

- Help buyers understand the buying process and educate them on current market conditions

- Help buyers to both understand that they will need to balance obtaining, and help them find, as many of their needs as possible, within the constraints of dealing with the realities of the market and / or their specific financial constraints

- Help buyers achieve their lifestyle needs with a different set of features than originally anticipated (this is particularly useful when dealing with financial constraints)

- Uncover and disclose any information that will help buyers make informed choices as to which properties to view and ultimately purchase.

- Help buyers in narrowing their search until they have identified their top choices through testing their criteria during the Buyers' Interview process.

- Advise buyers of clauses and pricing and help them understand the implications of the offer during the offer preparation phase.

- Manage the negotiation and counteroffer process so as to provide the client with the best possible advice in order for them to make the most informed decision.

- Provide oversight and follow up on any conditions to ensure the process proceeds as smoothly as possible and provide references to any service personnel that may be required.

What's your value in all this?

So what are buyers looking for from their REALTOR®? Since younger buyers are more likely to have never purchased a home before they're more likely to need assistance with understanding the process. According to the NAR study, all buyers benefit from their agent pointing out unnoticed features and faults in a property and all buyers most want their agent to help find the right home to purchase.

The study found that younger buyers valued the agent's honesty and trustworthiness as a significant factor and it's been shown as a result, that millennials tend not to be willing to sign Buyer Agreements with a REALTOR® until they've had the time to develop that trust.

Older buyers, however, rated the REALTOR's® reputation and their knowledge of the neighborhood as a higher factor. The study speculated that this may be due to older buyers tending to move longer distances and not necessarily knowing the neighborhood.

Referrals were the most common way that clients found their REALTOR®. Younger buyers predominantly used an agent that had been referred by a friend, neighbor, or relative, while older buyers were more likely to use an agent again that they previously used to buy or sell a home.

The study found that:

- Fifty-two percent of buyers found finding the right property the most difficult step.

- Twenty-four percent found understanding and completing the paperwork the most difficult part of the process.

- Fifteen percent of buyers had the most difficulty with understanding the complete process and what the next steps were

- Twelve percent found obtaining a mortgage the most difficult step.

The study went on to say that what buyers want most from their real estate agent is:

- Help finding the right home to purchase

- To help the buyer negotiate the terms of sale

- Help with the price negotiations

As can be seen, your value to this process is multifaceted and can be significant. Your involvement in the process, your skills and the team of support personnel you build, and to whom you can refer, will enable your buyer clients to find the right home, at the best possible price, with the best possible terms with the best guidance and information possible.

Who are they and where do they come from?

Buyers may come from many different sources. You can convert leads developed from ad and sign calls. Open houses, if well run, can be a great source of buyers. The most preferred source of leads is through referrals while prospecting is a necessary source of business. Sellers can also be a source of buyers. Running buyer or investor seminars is another outstanding opportunity to create buyer leads as are trade shows. In other words, buyers can be found wherever you decide to look for them.

When converting leads to buyers, you must have your lead follow-up system up and running and be ready to act immediately. It's important that you've developed and internalized your script so that you can easily convert a call to a lead and then to a buyer. Your script must allow you to qualify leads as you speak with them, as you don't want to waste time or gas with suspects or unmotivated people.

Ask and ye shall be given

Give and ye shall be broke! When speaking to a prospect, it's a give and take opportunity; you give them a little information, but it's critical that you get some back as well. As you're building rapport, remember to mirror the caller's tone, speed and volume. Answer their question then ask an open ended question to elicit some information that will help you grow your insight into what they're looking for and their motivation. Avoid closed ended questions. All you end up with is a yes or no answer.

"How much is the house?"

"It's $_____, is that the price range you were looking in?" Yes / No

Instead, try:

"It's $_____. What price range were you looking in?"

This leads them to provide more information and allows you ask more open ended questions as a follow up.

Caller: I'm calling about the house you're advertising for $_____. Can you tell me about it?"

"Sure. It's a 3 bedroom, 2 bathroom bungalow on a 50 by 150 lot. Can you tell me a little more about the kind of home you're looking for?"

"Can you tell me more about the specific community you want to move to?"

When describing the home, one of the key factors in getting buyers to become more interested in viewing it is to focus on the benefits of owning the home not just the features. People buy on emotion and then justify the purchase with logic, especially when the object is in demand. In order to appeal to that emotion, you need to be able to demonstrate to the prospect that there's some benefit to them of owning the home.

"It's a 3 bedroom, 2 bathroom bungalow on a 50 by 150 foot lot. Do you have kids? It's a great home for kids. They can play in the huge backyard. It's fully fenced so it's safe for them and there's plenty of room for them to run around. It's got a nice deck off the back so you can entertain and watch the kids play as well."

When I first started working as a REALTOR®, a trainer and coach in Edmonton named Lyndon Sommert demonstrated a great tool to use to pique the interest of potential buyers. It's called the Red File. Because that's what it is. It's a red file folder with a list of properties that you've previewed and believe are special due to their price or appeal. Having this file will allow you to maintain the conversation should the lead not find the home they're calling on appropriate for them.

"OK. It sounds like that house isn't for you, but I have a list of houses that I've seen that I think are great buys. Would you like to hear about them?"

This gives you the opportunity to create more curiosity, build more rapport with the caller and creates openings to close for an appointment.

Many times there is one consistent objection which crops up.

"Can you give me the address, I just want to drive by and take a look."

At this point you have a choice to make. You can give them the address and then hope they call you after they've looked at the house, or you can decide not to give them the address and close for an appointment. The first option leaves things to chance, the second eliminates it. They'll either agree to an appointment or they won't. If they don't, I would argue that they weren't serious in the first place and you're better not to have wasted your time.

Always try to close for the appointment using your objection handling skills, but if they insist on just getting the address, your answer should be, *"I understand that you would really like to drive by the home, but I only give out addresses to my clients."* Many times that answer will motivate them to agree to the appointment.

Informed Buyer's Guide

Once the prospect has agreed to the meeting, the next step in your lead follow up system must be to send them your Informed Buyer's Guide. This guide provides then information about you, such as:

- Who you are

- What you stand for (your Mission Statement) and what differentiates you from other agents

- Information about your brokerage

- Current market statistics

- The agency relationship

- The buyers' services you provide

- The buying process

- Testimonials

- A Buyer's Questionnaire

- Plain language versions of the contracts they'll encounter.

Once you've sent this, you then have an opportunity to follow up with them to find out if they've had a chance to read it, if they have any questions and can then reconfirm the meeting.

Business Building Exercise

Write out a list of qualifying questions you can use when you receive an ad or sign call and role play them with a colleague until you're comfortable with them.

Set up your Red File and begin previewing new listings.

Set up your Informed Buyers' Guide.

The First Meeting

Now that you've had the prospect agree to meeting with you, you can either bring them into the office or meet them in a public place such as a coffee shop. From a safety standpoint, it's much more preferable to meet where there are other people as opposed to having your first meeting with someone you don't know at the property or at their home.

At this meeting, your main task will be to find out about them. Using open ended questions you'll want to determine their needs and wants, their lifestyle and most importantly, their motivation.

You'll also want to demonstrate, by utilizing your Buyer's Presentation, how you can assist them throughout the buying process.

The Kick-Butt Buyer's Interview

Just as with the Listing Presentation, your Buyer's Interview has 4 key components:

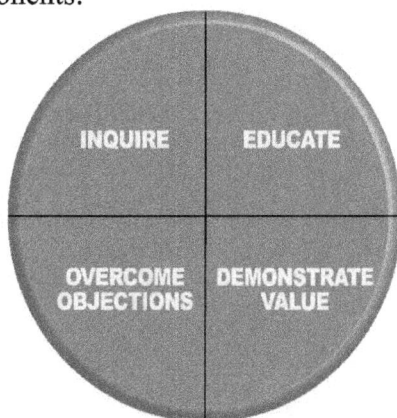

INQUIRE   EDUCATE

OVERCOME   DEMONSTRATE
OBJECTIONS   VALUE

A Silver Bullet

You can find a sample of the Informed Buyers Guide and Buyer's Presentation on the book's website www.foundationsforsuccess.ca.

The Inquiry

When working with buyers this component will likely be the most significant and lengthiest part of your Buyer's Interview. Here's where you get to find out as much information about the buyer as possible and, at the same time build rapport and ultimately find out how you can best serve the buyer's needs.

What kind of service are they looking for? The 2014 NAR Study revealed that the most difficult thing buyers faced was finding the right home, followed by understanding the paperwork involved. The majority wanted their REALTOR to help them find the home and then negotiate the terms and price for them. How involved do they want you to be in helping them through the process?

How do they want to communicate? It's important to know not just their method of communication, but how often they want to hear from you. How often do they expect to be in touch with you and what kind of information would they find most helpful?

What kind of buyer are they? Buyers come in many different shapes and sizes. There are first time buyers who are looking for a property to get them started on the road to a larger home. Others may want an investment that will appreciate after three to five years. They may be repeat buyers who may be looking for a house to meet their needs for the next ten to twenty years or investors looking for a good investment property with decent cash flow potential and an infinite number of other variables. Your job will be to ask the questions you need to in order to help you determine how to best serve their needs.

What kind of home are they looking for? Here again there's an infinite number of variables and this will be one of your major challenges. Unless you plan on spending a tremendous amount of time in your car, showing them every new home that's listed, you'll have to get them to be very specific about their ideal home. It's at this point in the interview where you'll utilize your Buyer's Questionnaire.

The Buyer's Questionnaire is designed, as part of the Buyer Management System, to help you ask the questions you need to in order to get the answers that will help point you in the right direction. It helps you clarify their Determinant Buying Motivation (DBM); what their main criteria for choosing a home is and what will sell them on a particular home. It assists in defining which houses to show them and which can be eliminated. However, the questionnaire is just a guide and doesn't include all the questions you'll need to ask. When you've asked a "What" question, it needs to be followed by a "Why" or clarifying question that will give you a better understanding of their true requirements.

"So, it sounds to me like you're looking for…is that right?"
Can you tell me a bit more about why that's important?"

For example, someone with an elderly parent and a couple of older children living with them may tell you that they need a bungalow, so the parent doesn't have to use any stairs. However, by asking the following clarifying question, you may gain more understanding of their true needs.

"I understand that you want to make sure your father doesn't have to use stairs. If I could find you a two storey home with a bedroom and bathroom on the main floor, would that work for you?"

19

Another situation that could arise would occur when a buyer tells you they want four bedrooms in the home. By asking the following question, you may be able to help them gain a better understanding of their options, which will ultimately help determine the homes to show them.

"You've said that you want four bedrooms. Would you consider a home with two or three bedrooms above grade and one or two in the basement?"

These questions may lead to further discussion and will ultimately help you home in on the right group of homes to show the buyers.

Once you've determined the right series of homes to show, your next major task will be to determine their motivation. This can best be determined by asking some key questions. These questions will help you determine if there is an urgency, an ability and a readiness to buy. If you have two of these three components in place it's fairly safe to say that you're dealing with a motivated buyer.

"Why are you thinking of buying?" This will help you better understand if there's there a compelling reason for the move or if they're just thinking about making a move. If there is a compelling reason, you've likely established that there's some urgency to the purchase as well as a readiness.

"Have you been pre-approved?" When potential buyers have taken the time to meet with a lender and gone through the paperwork required to be approved for a mortgage, you know they're serious about buying. If they're pre-approved, the ability

to buy exists, you know how what price range they're looking in and that they're indeed ready to buy.

"How long have you been looking?" *"Have you seen anything you really like?"* Motivated buyers generally don't take a long time to find a home. If your prospect has been looking for several months, they're probably not motivated enough for you to commit the one thing you can't waste, your time.

"When do you want to move / How soon do you plan on moving in?" This is similar to the previous question, in that it goes to a time frame for the move. However, where the first question asks how long they have been looking, this question seeks to find out how long they plan on looking. If they're not thinking of making a move within the next six months, it might be a better use of your time to put them on a drip email campaign and touch base with them every so often to see if their motivation has changed, rather than taking them out to homes that they're just not going to buy.

"If you found the right home today, would you be ready to buy it?" This is the ultimate qualifier question. If they answer with a yes, there's urgency, ability and a readiness to purchase.

"Are you working with a real estate agent?" While this doesn't have anything to do with their motivation, it's a critically important question to ask. Since you want to get paid for your work, asking this question will ensure that your efforts will be rewarded if you work with the buyers.

Some additional questions you may want to ask to assist in qualifying them are:

"If you could design the ideal moving situation for your family, what would it look like?"

"Do you need to sell your current home before you can buy?"

"Have you bought a property in the past?"

"Have you met with a lender yet? What Price Range are you looking in?"

"What can I do to make it easier for you to get the kind of real estate information you are looking for?"

"Tell me the process you typically use to make decisions like this?"

"What is the most important service you want from a real estate agent like myself?"

The Buyer Questionnaire – Page 1

BUYER QUESTIONNAIRE

Name: _____

Address: _____ Phone: _____

_____ Cell: _____

Email: _____ Fax: _____

Type of Property Wanted: Single Family House ☐ SF w/ Suite ☐   Condo ☐

Townhouse ☐   Detached ☐   Semi-Detached ☐   Attached/Row ☐

Area: **Central**   ☐   **North** ☐   **East** ☐   **West** ☐   **Out of Town** ☐

Neighbourhoods Desired _____

_____

Style: _____ Year: _____

Minimum Bdrms Up: _____   Minimum Bdrms Down: _____

Minimum Washrooms Up: _____   Minimum Washrooms Down: _____

Basement Development: P-Fin _____ F-Fin _____ Suite: _____ Suiteable: _____

Price Range: _____ Down Payment Available: _____

Garage: Yes ☐   No ☐   Single ☐   Double ☐   Larger ☐

Amenities Desired: _____

_____

Pre-approved: Y   N   Bank: _____   Int. Rate: _____

Willing to do upgrades: Y   N   How Much: _____

Other Important Info:

The Buyer Questionnaire – Page 2

ADDITIONAL QUESTIONS

Is the age of the home important? _____

What are you looking for in a kitchen, family room? _____

_____

Do you want a separate dining room? _____

What is your preferred layout? _____

What are your high priority features: appliances, ensuite, fireplace?

_____

_____

What other types of rooms do you need? A main floor laundry, a home office?

_____

_____

What about storage space? Basements, lockers?

_____

_____

Is energy efficiency important? Newer windows or a high efficiency furnace?

_____

_____

What other landscaping features are important: a fenced yard, play areas, pool, gardens?

_____

_____

Is the direction the home faces important? _____

Educate the Buyer

There's a wide range of misinformation about the market, what REALTORS® do and a multiplicity of other issues. As part of your Buyer Interview, it will be your responsibility to find out what information the buyer has and what they don't. You'll need to spend some time reviewing that information and correcting any misunderstandings they may have. You'll also need to educate them on the information they don't have; provide them with answers to the things they don't know that they don't know.

They'll need to be shown the realities of the overall market for the area as well as the community in which they wish to live. You'll need to explain how the inventory levels and seller expectations may affect the prices and potential for multiple offers.

There's a commonly held misconception that, should the Buyer work with the listing representative, they may get a break on the price due to a possible reduction in the agent's commission. It's important that you educate them on the roles, responsibilities and fiduciary duties of the Seller's Representative vs. the Buyers' Representative.

Since the Listing Sales Representative is under contract with the seller to market and sell their property for the best possible price the buyer needs to understand that the Seller's Representative's primary responsibility is to their client, the Seller. When a buyer contacts the Seller's Representative, they should be aware that a listing agent can only be expected to:

• Arrange a showing.

• Help arrange financing.

- Provide details about the property.

- Explain all the forms and agreements related to buying the property.

They should not, therefore, expect the listing representative to discuss anything related to the sellers' motivation to sell or the price that the seller will accept.

They should also understand that the amount of the commission is between the Sales Representative and the seller and that any break in the commission will benefit the seller, not the buyer. In other words, the buyer is not assured of getting a reduced price if they work with the listing representative; rather, the seller will likely end up netting more.

However, when the buyer engages the services of their own personal Sales Representative, someone who is under contract to work solely in their best interest, they get all of the same services listed above plus:

- A Sales Representative that will look after their needs first.

- All the applicable fiduciary duties with no possibility of any conflicts of interest.

- Access to all available listings rather than just the one they called on.

- Expert advice, when writing an offer, on including clauses which will provide the best protection for the client including home inspections, financing and many others.

- Expert negotiation of the offer to purchase so as to achieve the best possible price and terms for the buyer rather than the seller.

- Expert advice on market value and pricing, as well as helping them decide when they should consider walking away from the negotiation.

- Discovery and disclosure of any available information about the property including liens, warranties, disclosures, seller's purchase price, and market and planning activity in the area.

Part of educating the buyer is also to review the buying process from start to finish. In doing so, you can ensure that they understand each step, who is responsible for what and what the next step will be.

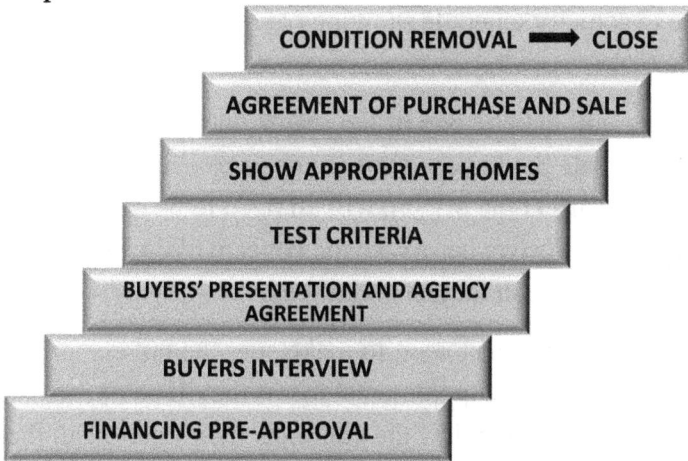

CONDITION REMOVAL ➡ CLOSE

AGREEMENT OF PURCHASE AND SALE

SHOW APPROPRIATE HOMES

TEST CRITERIA

BUYERS' PRESENTATION AND AGENCY AGREEMENT

BUYERS INTERVIEW

FINANCING PRE-APPROVAL

Now that they've been pre-approved and everyone is aware of the price range in which they should be searching, the next stage is to really determine the type of home and location to look at. You'll need to educate them on the Buyer Representation Agreement (or whatever the Buyer Contract is called in your jurisdiction) and how it can ensure that you're acting in their best interest. If they're ready, you can then get them to sign it at this point.

Testing, Testing...

The next step will be to search for the homes they've described and "test" their criteria, by conducting a search on MLS for the homes that match those criteria. This will allow you to confirm that the type of home, with the features, in the price range and the area they've described, is available. This will also allow you or the buyer to make any modifications to their criteria based on having viewed the homes online, and will save both you and the buyer time, by eliminating the need to drive around to view homes that wouldn't have matched their wants and needs. The next step will be to actually schedule showings of homes that do match their criteria.

Pricing will also be one of the major items upon which you'll need to educate the buyer. How home prices are determined and what factors affect the pricing will all need to be discussed at this point so that the buyer has a realistic concept of the price of homes in the areas in which they intend to buy.

The next item you'll want to make sure the buyers understand are the contracts and supplemental forms they'll come into contact with. It's helpful to review the contracts thoroughly with them so there are no surprises along the way.

It's also advisable to let them know how negotiations work and what kind of expenses they can expect to incur, including legal costs, deposits, land transfer taxes, and adjustments. Remember, the better educated your clients are, the fewer problems there can be with the sale process.

And the final aspect of the process will be educating them on the different conditions that they may encounter when writing a purchase agreement, what they mean and how they can affect the buyer. Explaining who will be involved in managing them and how they will be removed will also help reduce the possibility of issues cropping up at a later stage.

Demonstrate Your Value

This is the part where you get to distinguish yourself from the other REALTORS® they may have been speaking with. Here's where you get to talk about the benefits of your services, and how you're going to meet the needs they expressed in the inquiry phase of your meeting and how you can do that better than anyone else. It's not about the number of services you can provide, it's about the benefits the client will receive from using your services and the value they perceive that you bring to the table.

The simplest way to do that is to review each of their needs and then explain how you will meet them.

"Mr. and Mrs. Buyer, we spoke about how important responsiveness was to you. Here's how I provide that kind of service to my clients...."

"Mr. and Mrs. Buyer, you said that working with someone who has knowledge of the buying process was very important. Let me show you how I can provide that to you."

Overcome Objections

Throughout the inquiry phase, by asking loads of open ended questions, you're going to find out what kind of concerns the buyers may have. This phase of the buyer's interview allows you to review those concerns and deal with them before they crop up as actual objections. As you move through the interview it's important to check back with the buyers and make sure they understand each step.

"Mr. and 'Mrs. Buyer, now that we've had a chance to discuss...How does that sound?"

"Does that make sense?"

"Do you have any questions about what we just discussed?"

Asking these questions and then providing them with the answers to their concerns now, will save you many headaches when it comes time to try to help them make the decision to write an offer later.

A fully educated buyer, who understands the value that you bring to the transaction, is one who is able to make better informed decisions, who will recognize that you're the REALTOR® they want to work with and who will, ultimately, be an easier client with whom to work.

CHAPTER 2

The Buyers' System

The very first step in managing a complete buyers' system has to be working with buyers who are motivated and ready to buy. We've all had the experience of working with buyers who aren't at that point yet, and it becomes a sequence of taking people out to homes that don't truly fit their needs or aren't the "right house" over and over again.

This goes back to your lead follow up system and your ability to qualify leads. Are they a true lead, a warm or a cold prospect?

Without a comprehensive system which ensures a consistent approach to all the activities involved, it becomes very easy to inadvertently miss something that may at first seem trivial, but can eventually become a major issue. For example, when writing an offer, it may seem like overkill to pull the title on a property to confirm who the sellers are. After all, the listing agent would have done that, right? However, what happens if there's an error in the listing information and the spelling of the sellers' name is incorrect? That little error, if not corrected, will become a major issue later on. By following the same process and procedure every time, for every person, you can safeguard yourself against even minor slips.

A thorough buyers' system begins with the buyer's file. Once you've established that the prospect is a qualified, motivated buyer, their information is placed in a file which will include the following:

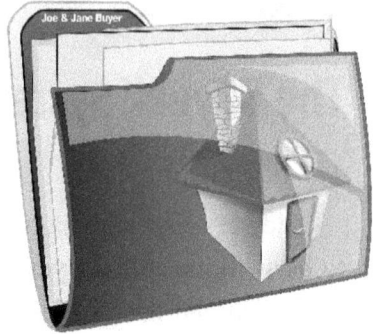

- The Buyer's Task List, which includes:

    - The buyer's complete contact information

    - The contact information of their mortgage broker and lawyer

    - The dates of any offers and conditions relating to it

- The Buyer Questionnaire and any supporting notes, which will provide the criteria the buyer has used to determine the homes to be considered.

- Copies of all the listings you've shown them

- A copy of any Purchase Contracts, whether accepted or not, and supporting documents such as:

    - Schedules, Amendments, Waivers and / or Notices of Fulfillment, Mutual Releases, etc.

- A copy of the title for any purchase contracts written

- A copy of the deposit cheque and receipt for any accepted offers

- The buyers' CMA which can be used to help justify the purchase price offered when dealing with offers.

- The signed Buyer Representation Agreement (BRA)

- All necessary FINTRAC forms

- Any correspondence with the client and any other REALTOR® regarding the purchase

- The Deal Tracking Form, a detailed list of everything required to be completed once an offer has been accepted, including:

  - The offer date

  - The closing date

  - The Seller's name

  - The Seller's REALTOR® name and contact info

  - The Seller's lawyer name and contact info

  - The Buyer's lawyer name and contact info

  - The amount of the deposit, the date and time it was delivered to the listing office

  - Any conditions, when they are to be removed and the dates when they are actually removed

  - Any additional terms of the contract

- A copy of the commission cheque stub in case it's needed for tax purposes.

This file should be carried with you, in either a paper or electronic format, so you have it readily at hand should any issues crop up.

The Buyer Task List

BUYER'S TASK LIST

MLS#:		OFFER DATE:			CONDITION DATE:	
INSPECTION DATE:				POSSESSION DATE:		
Address:						
Client Name:						
Residence Phone:				Cell:		
Business Phone:				Business Fax:		
Email Address:						
Lawyer's Name:						
Phone:				Fax:		
Mortgage Broker:				Phone:		Fax:

ITEM		ATTACHED TO FILE	
PURCHASE CONTRACT:			
Purchase Contract signed		Accepted Purchase Contract	
Purchase Contract presented		MLS Feature Sheet	
Purchase Contract accepted		Tax Assessment Form	
Initial Deposit cheque copied		Survey if available	
Initial Deposit cheque to Listing Realtor		GeoWarehouse Printout	
Purchase Contract faxed to Mortgage Broker		Property History	
Receipt confirmed		Copy of Initial Deposit	
		Copy of Additional Deposit (if needed)	
Trade Record Sheet Submitted w/ copies of:		Copy of Trade Record Sheet	
• Purchase Contract		Buyer's Representation Agreement	
• Deposit Cheque		Working with a REALTOR	
• MLS Feature Sheet		Confirmation of Cooperation &	
• BRA		Representation	
• Working with a REALTOR		Individual Identification (FINTRAC)	
• Confirmation of Cooperation & Rep.		Receipt of Funds (FINTRAC)	
• Individual Identification (FINTRAC)			
• Receipt of Funds (FINTRAC)			
CONDITIONS:		**FOLLOW UP:**	
Inspection Booked		1 day	
Inspection Condition Removed		1 week	
Check with Mortgage Broker 2 days prior		1 month	
Financing Condition Removed		Clients transferred to Database	
Review of Status Certificate Removed		Set up on Newsletter	
Condition Removal faxed to Listing Realtor		24 Touch System instituted	
Additional Deposit copied (if needed)			
Additional Deposit to Listing Realtor			
1 WEEK PRIOR TO POSSESSION:			
Call Lawyer to confirm			
Call Listing REALTOR to confirm possession			
Call Clients			
Schedule final buyer's walkthrough			
DAY OF POSSESSION:			
Call Lawyer to confirm Key Release			
Call Listing Realtor to confirm Key Release			
Call Clients – Meet at new home for walkthrough			

A Silver Bullet

You can find a copy of the forms and checklists in this chapter at www.foundationsforsuccess.ca.

Business Building Exercise

Set up a number of Buyer files with all the paperwork required by your brokerage, your Buyer's Task List, Buyer's Questionnaire and Deal Tracking Form and have them ready for when you begin taking buyers out on showings.

On the Road Again

The next component of the buyer system is your method of managing showings. When showing homes, I've found it helpful to provide the buyers with basic guidelines of how I handle the showings, using the following **"Rules of the Road"**.

1. Each time we view homes, I'll prepare a list of the homes along with a map for you to follow from one home to the next. (Thank goodness for Google Maps). You'll also get a copy of the listing information for each home.

2. I try to book our showings in one hour sessions for each home. This is done so that we have the time to spend viewing each house and allows us to run a bit behind schedule, without creating any inconvenience for the homeowners at our next showing.

3. Please be on time for the first showing. This will help us stay on schedule. Remember, the home owners will have had to leave the home and we want to make sure we don't create any more disruption to their routine than we have to.

4. If you are going to be late, please give me at least 15 minutes' notice so I can notify the listing agent who can then inform his clients.

5. When going through homes, please be prepared to remove your footwear. After all, we don't want to track stuff through someone's house.

6. As you go through each home, feel free to open any closets, cupboards and behind every door. If this is going to be your home, you need to know what everything looks like.

7. I would suggest that as we view the homes, you may want to make notes about each one for future reference. That will help you distinguish the homes you like from the ones you don't.

8. Please stay together as you go through the home, especially if you have children. That will reduce any chance of accidents or injury to anyone.

9. If you need to use the washroom during the visit, please check with me first. We may occasionally encounter a home where the water will have been shut off and we don't want to have that kind of problem, do we?

10. Please hold any negative comments until we get out of the home. We don't want to take the chance on anything getting back to the seller which we don't want them to hear.

11. Most sellers want to know what you thought of the home. I believe in providing feedback that will help people get their home sold, even if not to you. Please let me know what you like and don't like about the homes we view so I can give those comments to the listing REALTOR® when they ask.

Home Showing System

In order to ensure you don't create confusion for your buyers it's advisable to show a maximum of four to five homes each time you take them out. Since you don't want to waste their time or yours, the homes MUST be compatible with the requirements decided on at the first meeting.

When booking showings, call the listing REALTOR®'s office at least one day prior to the scheduled showing to ensure that you get confirmation of the showing. This is absolutely necessary when the listing requires 24 hours' notice. The method of booking showings varies widely across the country and is beyond the scope of this book.

Business Building Exercise

Check with your broker or manager for the specifics of booking showings in your area.

In order to avoid wasting time when showing properties, it's advisable to use a mapping system such as Google Maps or the one built into your MLS system to map out the homes. Arrange the showings in a logical sequence and then book the showings based on the travel time between each. The system I've always found that works best is to book each showing for one hour, but stagger the showings by half an hour. In other words, home 1 is scheduled between 2:00 – 3:00, home 2 between 2:30 – 3:30, home 3 between 3:00 – 3:30, etc. I provide the clients with a copy of the map with the directions between each property as well as the client view of the MLS listing sheet in the order of the showings with the showing times on each.

Once you've arrived at the property, try to find something small that's wrong with the property while you and the clients are walking to it. This tends to go a long way in demonstrating that you're on their side.

When entering the property, ring the doorbell and, when you open the door, announce your presence. Many years ago, I was showing a home to a female buyer and had to take my younger daughter with me. I had booked the showing the day before and it had been confirmed that no one was going to be home during the showing. When we arrived and based on the information I had received that no-one would be home, I skipped my usual habit of opening the door and calling out "Hello!" a couple of times. I opened the door and we proceeded down the hall. As we did, the door to the bathroom at the end of the hall opened and out stepped a very naked young man. Needless to say, everyone was somewhat startled and embarrassed and I learned a valuable lesson.

When touring the home, part of my system is to have the clients wait at the front door while I turn on the lights and then follow them through the home, so as to allow the clients to discover the home themselves; to have that "WOW" moment. By not leading them, it also prevents you from introducing them to the various rooms; *"This is the living room, this is the kitchen ...".* Honestly, if they don't know that the room with the fridge and stove is the kitchen, they probably shouldn't be buying a home.

As you proceed through the home, an important part of showing buyers through the home is to relate what they told you they were looking for to the benefits of the home. *"Didn't you say you wanted...Would this home would work well for that?"* Should they have any questions about the structure or concerns about the house, remind them that, *"That's why we're going to have an inspection done."*

One of the key things to remember about any questions the buyer may ask is to know what you know and what you don't. Don't assume, don't try to bluff; answer their questions honestly. It's OK to let them know you don't know the answer, but that you will find out the answer for them.

Once you've finished the showing, ask for feedback, don't give it. The last thing you want is to do is to talk yourself out of a sale. Despite your belief that this is definitely not the home for them, let the buyers make up their own mind.

In order to help determine the buyer's feelings about the home, use trial closes throughout the showing and listen for clues in what they're saying. If she turns to him and says, *"You know, our living room furniture would look really good in here,"* it's a great indication that this is one of the homes under serious consideration. You may, at this point, want to test the waters and find out what they're thinking.

"So folks, let me ask. What do you think about this home?"

"So, how does this home stack up?"

"Can you see yourself living here?"

After you've completed the showing, one of the most important steps you'll take is to ask for the sale. This is the point where many REALTORS® get cold feet and lose out on possible sales. Your trial closes will indicate if they've found a home they like and if you don't ask for a decision, they may not make one.

Sometimes, the buyer is actually waiting for you to ask for the decision and won't make one without you asking. Always ask them for a decision. As Wayne Gretzky once said, *"You miss 100 percent of the shots you don't take."*

> *"It sounds to me like this is a home you really like. So what do you think about writing an offer on it?"*

> *"Would you like to sit down and discuss the purchase of this home?"*

> *"If you feel this is the home for you let's go back to my office and I'll do a Comparative Market Analysis so you'll have some information to base an offer price on."*

At this point you have three possible options, depending on the buyers' response. You can write the offer. If they haven't found the right home, you can have them sign a Buyer Representation Agreement and continue to work with them or, if they aren't prepared to sign a BRA, you can either continue to work with them on the chance they won't sign an offer with another REALTOR® or you can let them know you only work with people who have signed a BRA and let them go.

The Buyers from Hell? It may not be them

Many years ago, I had the opportunity to work with a client who, it seemed, was bound and determined to do everything they could to frustrate every deal I wrote for them. There was always something wrong with the way the house was priced, or the layout of the home was wrong, or something on the inspection was too serious for them to move forward with the purchase. During the American Revolution, Thomas Paine wrote, "These are the times that try men's souls." And this was the client who tried my patience, to the point that I finally gave up on them, only to later learn they had then bought a home with another REALTOR® on the first time out.

We've all had the "Buyer from Hell"; the client who, no matter how hard you work, no matter how many homes you show them, no matter how many offers you write for them, just don't seem to get the concept of what it's going to take to actually buy a home. Or they complain about everything and seem to throw up roadblocks at every turn in the process. Well, maybe it's not actually them.

It's important to remember that, many times, these folks may not be sure of the process, what's involved, who's responsible for what and what to expect when they go out and look at homes with a REALTOR®. They're probably under some stress and that generally doesn't bring out the best in people. Your job will be to help them, for the most part, alleviate that stress.

In order to accomplish that, you're going to need to understand them and to empathize with them; to put yourself in their place. Since, as REALTORS®, looking at homes, writing and negotiating offers and understanding the process is old hat to us, it's easy to overlook or miss the uncertainty and stress that can cause even the calmest client to lose their equanimity. Our responsibility goes far beyond simply finding and securing them a home. We need to understand who they are, how they communicate, to understand their concerns, where they're unsure, what their motivation is and to make sure we've educated and advised them so as to reduce or eliminate any of the issues which can cause them discomfort throughout the process.

I would argue that, in many cases, the buyer from hell is simply a reflection of our own failings in the communication, empathy and objection handling departments. All too often we try to "sell" something to our clients, whether it be ourselves and our services or a property; in essence, we try to provide solutions to them.

Where we tend to get it wrong, though, is when we try to offer a solution we think will resolve the problem, without actually spending the time to find out what the real, deep down, pain actually is. We know that, for the most part, people buy because of pain. They either want to eliminate it or avoid it. It used to be a statute of sales that to sell something we had to offer a solution to the problem. I would suggest, instead of offering up solutions, we need to look at sales as if we are doctors. We need to find out about their pain. In my previous career, I learned a really helpful mnemonic that used to help me ask questions about my patients' problem. That mnemonic was WOCSNOR and it goes like this:

W What's your WORST pain? In other words, what's the most important issue they're facing in their current situation? Is it money, space, location or something else?

O What OTHER pain is there? Is there something else that's creating an issue for them in their current location? What's the next most important thing?

C Is it CONSTANT or INTERMITTENT? In other words, is this something that's a constant problem they need to get away from right now, or does it create problems on an occasional basis they would like to move away from?

S How SIGNIFICANT is the pain? Is this situation untenable or can they live with it if they have to?

N What's the NATURE of the pain? What is the actual pain the client is experiencing and feel needs to be resolved? This is where your ability to ask questions and actively listen will earn you the respect and trust of the client.

O Are there any OTHER symptoms? These are things other than the pain which are creating issues for them and that they feel need to be resolved.

R What's the RELATIONSHIP of the pain and the symptoms? If the pain gets worse, do the symptoms?

A simple example of this may be that the client has a problem in keeping up with their current mortgage (their worst pain). As a consequence, they are having to work longer hours which is placing a strain on their family life (other pain). Since they feel under stress all the time, the problem is constantly with them and is taking a significant toll on them and their family. They believe the large mortgage is just too much for them to continue to support and that having a smaller mortgage will remove the issue (the nature of the pain). They feel, since there is an increased strain on the family, they're seeing more behavioural difficulties for the kids in school (other symptoms) and as the issue becomes worse so do the resultant behaviours.

Now, I know this sounds a lot like pop psychology, and in this example, it probably is. And the solution for this, from our perspective, is easy; sell the current house and buy a less expensive one. However, if you take this kind of approach to finding out what the problem is, then explore different lines of inquiry, and finally, help them understand that the cost created by the problem exceeds the cost of making a change, you can then offer your clients different solutions to the problem. For example, they may be able to refinance the existing home to ease the mortgage pressure. They may be able to take in tenants to defray some of the costs. And perhaps, they may want to consider the sale and purchase option. In any case, by finding out about the pain, giving them options and then helping them to deal with the solutions, you eliminate a significant portion of the fear, confusion and pain that leads them to become the buyers' from hell.

Let's Write an Offer

What a wonderful phrase! But, now comes the real challenge. It's at this point that your knowledge of contracts, the market, objection handling, offer presentation and negotiation gets put to the test.

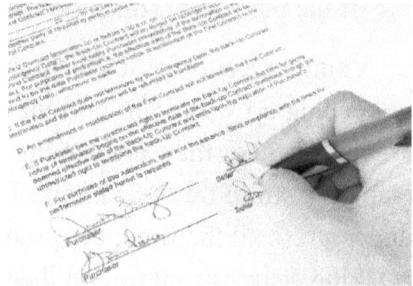

The first step in the whole process is to explain the different types of representation. In Ontario, these are single, multiple representation and customer status. Make sure you familiarize yourself with the ones in your area, so you can explain them thoroughly to the buyer.

If you haven't already got them signed, the next step is to have the buyers sign the applicable representation agreements and any other required forms (if applicable).

The next step is to prepare a buyer's Comparative Market Analysis so that the buyers can understand the way homes are priced in the area. You'll also want to have as much market information, such as past and present trends and patterns, as possible to back up the CMA when you explain it to your client and when it comes time to negotiate for them.

One of the most common questions you can expect to get is *"What do you think we should offer?"* You can offer information based on your experience and expertise, but should avoid advising the client on the actual price to offer. Provide them with a price range, but make sure they're the ones to name the price they want to pay. In this way, you can avoid any question of misrepresentation of the price.

When writing the offer, explain the forms, clauses and schedules as you go. This will ensure your client fully understands the entire contract and has the opportunity to ask any questions they may have about what's involved. Offers to purchase are made up of five major factors:

- Price
- Conditions

- Terms

- Chattels and Fixtures

- Possession date

You'll need to explain how the structuring of each component can help or hinder the buyers' chances of getting the offer accepted with as few changes as possible. Ensure they understand the possible consequence of writing a low offer. These may be alienating the seller, resulting in an outright rejection of the offer or a counter offer at, or close to, the list price. The seller may refuse to deal with another offer from the buyer, should they decide to write another one and they take the risk of another offer coming in, forcing them into a multiple offer.

You'll want to ensure the chattels and fixtures specified in the offer match those in the listing and that all exclusions are identified as well.

We'll Take It If...

Our most important task, our primary duty, is to protect the interests of our client. Many times clients will rely on your knowledge and advice on what to include in an offer; however, there will be occasions when they want a property so much that they're willing to forgo some of the protections offered by including specific conditions in an offer. It's your responsibility to advise them of the desirability of having a condition that protects them and the consequences of not including that clause.

While this section is not meant in any way to be a comprehensive guide to the conditions which should be included in an offer, there are certain conditions which, if ignored, can have serious consequences for both the buyer and their REALTOR®.

Your job will be to determine which will best protect your client and help them make the best possible informed decision about which to include. As a new REALTOR® you're strongly advised to seek the advice of your manager or Broker about which conditions you may want to include in any offers you write. It's in your best interest, and your clients', to have your manager check the first few offers you write to make sure you've included everything you need and that everything's in order before having the clients sign them.

Review and ask for agreement on each condition and term. In the event the buyer chooses not to include a recommended condition, you may want to consider having them sign a form which acknowledges you've advised them to include it, but they have chosen not to. In Ontario that form is the Acknowledgement re: Conditions in Offer (Form 127).

One of the most important conditions is that of financing. The potential consequences of not including a financing condition are extreme. Imagine someone who buys a home without such a condition, only to find out later that they can't actually afford the home. Not only will they lose their deposit, but they could potentially be on the hook for any damages incurred by the seller when they have to resell the home again. These damages could include the difference between the price the buyer agreed to pay and the new sale price if it's less, the carrying costs for the home over the period of time it takes to resell, and many more.

The next and, in my opinion, equally important condition is that of the property inspection. Failure to include this condition has the potential for very serious consequences. While we're all very aware about the necessity of disclosing latent defects, there are times when even the seller may not have knowledge of issues which could create a problem. Should your buyer purchase a home without having an inspection completed, they're putting themselves at risk for some nasty surprises. Buying a home is expensive enough without having to come up with even more money as a result of any unpleasant surprises.

Another issue commonly faced nowadays is the presence of rental items, such as hot water heaters, furnaces, security systems and others, which carry a rental contract with them. Some of these contracts can carry onerous cancellation or transfer provisions in them. In order to protect your buyer from accepting what could be onerous terms, the inclusion of a condition in which the buyer has the opportunity to review the rental agreements is one which must be considered.

Business Days vs. Date and Time

One of the most common ways in which condition removal can become an issue is the use of the term 'business days' when defining a date a condition is to be satisfied. In most contracts, business days are specified as any day, other than Saturday, Sunday or statutory holidays in the applicable Province. Sounds pretty clear, doesn't it? Let's take a closer look at the term and the possible implications.

The "Business Day" is typically considered to cover the period from 9 a.m. to 5 p.m. However, this is simply a convention and may cause some uncertainty as to when a condition must be waived or fulfilled. Another concern which may arise is when the term of days is to begin. Let's assume an offer has a condition that requires removal within five business days. If the offer is accepted at 10 pm, it makes sense that the five days would begin on the following morning, as no business could reasonably be transacted for the remainder of the day. If the offer was accepted on a Monday, the conditions could reasonably be expected to be removed on the following Monday. However, if the offer was accepted at 9 am on the Monday, it could be argued that there was a reasonable expectation that business could be transacted throughout the remainder of that day, leading to an expectation that condition removal should occur by Friday of the same week. This could, therefore, lead to an issue if both parties are not of the same mindset.

In order to eliminate the possibility of this uncertainty arising, it's advisable to clearly define when the condition must be waived or fulfilled. This can best be done by using a specific date and time for condition removal.

"Unless the Buyer gives notice in writing delivered to the Seller personally or in accordance with any other provisions for the delivery of notice in this Agreement of Purchase and Sale or any Schedule thereto not later than _____ p.m. on _____, that this condition is fulfilled, this Offer shall be null and void and the deposit shall be returned to the Buyer in full without deduction."

While this may require a few changes and initials during the negotiation process, the little extra work involved will eliminate the possibility of even more work being required if there is uncertainty about removal date as well as the possibility of the transaction failing as a result.

One thing to remember when writing an offer is that the possession or closing date should not be on a weekend or a holiday. I've also tried to avoid setting the closing on a Friday or on the last day of the month. I avoid Fridays in case there's a delay in getting the funds transferred. If that happens, the buyer could end up not having a home to move into over the weekend, which could make for very unhappy clients. Also, try booking a mover for the last day of the month, unless you've booked four months in advance.

Make certain that all the chattels and fixtures your clients want, as well as the exclusions listed, have been clearly stated, don't take anything for granted. If you're not certain what constitutes a fixture or a chattel, my colleague and friend Brian Madigan has a simple solution. He says to, *"Imagine picking up the property and turning it upside down. Anything that falls out is a chattel and anything that doesn't is a fixture."* That's the best description I've heard yet.

Once everything has been completed, your next task is take a few minutes and review each page of the offer to make sure that all the signatures and initials are in place. Time spent now will more than make up for the time you'll have to spend running around to get a missed signature or initial.

Request an appropriate deposit and explain how it will assist in demonstrating to the seller that the buyers are serious about purchasing the home and in getting the offer accepted.

Throughout the offer process you may, if they're going to occur, encounter some objections from the buyer. We'll discuss handling these objections in the volume titled "I'm Just Sayin'"

In the event that your offer is part of a multiple offer, you'll need to advise your client on the multiple offer process and how they can best position their offer for success.

The Offer Process

Whether you're in a single or a multiple offer, your primary responsibility is protect your client's best interests.

Remember, and remind the buyer, you're there to advise, but the decisions are theirs to make, not yours, and that you are bound by their lawful and ethical instructions.

When dealing with a single offer, your offer management system must ensure, once the offer has been signed, you inform the listing REALTOR® that you have an offer for them. This may take different forms in different jurisdictions. For example, in Ontario, this means calling the listing office and registering the offer. However, no matter which format is used in your area, the most important component is to speak directly with the listing REALTOR® so as to ensure there's no opportunity for miscommunication. Once that has occurred, a time for the offer presentation should be established.

Never discuss the offer over the phone. This only provides the opportunity for the listing REALTOR® to begin preparing to counter your offer and weakens your position. At the time of the offer presentation it may be beneficial to have the buyers close by so that any counter offers can be dealt with rapidly. I've had clients sitting outside the property in their car or at a nearby coffee shop.

At the offer presentation, your job is to try to build rapport with the Sellers, so as to help them better understand your clients and to help your clients obtain the best possible terms. Provide some information about the buyers. What are their motives for wanting the house? What have they said about the house to show they appreciate its features and benefits? Respond to questions and concerns from the sellers and be prepared to handle any objections which may occur.

Remember that facts and figures are persuasive; arguing and too much talk are usually ineffective. Very often sellers and buyers are ready to accept the terms of an offer but need a rationale and this is where all the work you have done in the building trust stage and determining needs will pay off. Make sure you are prepared to offer the objective support that they need.

If you obtain a counteroffer from the sellers, you have another offer to sell and it becomes the buyers' option to accept, reject or counter. When negotiating the counteroffer, your objective is to help the buyers understand the changes and why they're important to the sellers. This will help your clients make an informed decision about what they want to do with the counteroffer. Finally, be patient. Don't push. Ask questions, watch the buyers' body language, let them sell themselves on the counteroffer.

Once the offer has been accepted, make sure any changes have been initialled and final signatures have been completed.

Your next task will be to make copies of the agreement, the deposit cheque and the receipt for the deposit and provide a copy to your buyers and the office, as well as place a copy in your buyers' file.

Multiple Offer Management

Dealing with multiple offers can be frustrating and challenging. Your job will be to give your client the best chance to win the war. There are six key factors to success in this, including:

- Mindset & Preparation

- Price

- Conditions

- Terms

- Dates

- Deposit

Mindset & Preparation

Clients may face the specter of entering into multiple offer situations many times, which can become a frustrating experience; one which may actually deter some buyers from proceeding further with their plans to purchase. In an effort to reduce this frustration, it's important to explain the multiple offer process to prepare them for the possibility and educate them on what it takes to win.

Should you find yourselves in a multiple offer, you'll need to explore their motivation and determine what their mindset is regarding the price they're offering.

"You said that your best offer is $X. If the house sold for $X plus $2,000, would you be okay with that or would you have paid the extra $2,000 to get the house?"

Price

Of course, one of the major factors affecting a seller's decision about which offer to go with is the price. You'll need to help your client establish their top dollar and not let them fall into an auction mentality. Set your target and don't go beyond it. The most important thing you can do to assist them with this decision is to do your homework; provide them with a complete CMA. You must have your facts and figures ready and review current sales. Prior to showing homes, and definitely before writing an offer, it's necessary to speak with their financing person and find out their maximum approved price. This will help ensure they understand their limits and avoid the auction knee jerk reaction.

Conditions

While price will play a major part in the decision, winning in a multiple offer is not just about the price. It's also about conditions; the number and content of them.

Remember, your job is to protect your client's interests, so including conditions will certainly accomplish that. However, try to keep them to a minimum and as simple as possible, with as short a period for removal as possible. Your clients may elect to write the offer with no conditions. In this event, you'll need to discuss this with them and make sure they understand the potential consequences of having no conditions in the offer. Should they choose to continue, ensure you've had them sign the form discussed earlier.

When including a financing condition, you'll want to ensure the client is pre-approved and that both you and they know their maximum limit.

Including an inspection condition is extremely important in order to protect your client. However, you may be able to eliminate it by having an advance home inspection completed. This will allow your client to completely understand the issues in the house and to determine if they want to continue with the offer. This, however, can become expensive, since the inspection may cost your client around $400-500, with no assurance they may want to move forward or, if they do, that they'll actually end up winning the multiple offer.

One option to consider was suggested to me by Brian Madigan. It's to include an inspection condition in which the buyer will "absorb" the first $X of any deficiencies found on the inspection. This clause states that the buyer will accept any minor flaws in the home, up to a specified amount of repairs, but that should anything serious be found, they have the right not to proceed.

"This Offer is conditional upon the Buyer, at the Buyer's own expense, having the relevant building(s) inspected by a bona fide home inspection firm to determine that the building(s) are in sound structural and mechanical condition and that the electrical system is safe and adequate, and that, in the written opinion of the home inspection firm, all deficiencies can be remedied at a cost not greater than _____ (\$ _____). Unless the Buyer gives notice in writing delivered to the Seller personally or in accordance with any other provisions for the delivery of notice in this Agreement of Purchase and Sale or any Schedule thereto not later than 8:00 p.m. on the _____ day of _____ 20___, that this condition is fulfilled, this Offer shall be null and void and the deposit shall be returned to the Buyer in full without deduction. The Seller agrees to co-operate in providing access to the property for the purpose of this inspection. The Seller agrees this condition is included for the benefit of the Buyer and may be waived at the Buyer's sole option by notice in writing to the Seller as aforesaid within the time period stated herein."

Terms

Keep any terms to minimum and make sure there's nothing onerous in them that may create an issue for the sellers. Don't ask for random items, such as the lawnmower or snow blower. Include the chattels and fixtures as shown on the listing.

One of the most common terms included is that of having the seller leave the house in a clean and broom swept condition and remove all debris from the house and yard. When going into a multiple offer, you may want to consider changing that to say the "Buyer will clean the house". This can be very appealing, as sellers want to concentrate on packing and moving and don't want to have to worry about having to take the extra step of having the home cleaned.

Dates

The simplest option here is to give the sellers their closing date. If there are conditions present, keep the dates as tight as possible.

Deposit

Try using a larger deposit to demonstrate to the seller that the buyer is serious about completing the transaction. It's easier to walk away from a $5,000 deposit than it is a much larger one. Here's an example:

Offer 1	Offer 2
$450,000 offer	$450,000 offer
80% financing = $360,000	80% financing = $360,000
5% deposit = $22,500	Deposit = $90,000
Cash to Close = $67,500	No cash to close

No conditions   No conditions

Offers 1 and 2 provide the same price and terms, however, Offer 2 demonstrates much more commitment to completing the transaction and may help sway the sellers.

Buyer's Letter

The use of a Buyer's Letter may help to sway the sellers. Sellers are often emotional about selling their home and will often identify with a buyer who loves their home for the same reasons that they do. Have your buyers write a cover letter to the sellers telling them a little something about every member of the family, including the children and what it is about their home that makes them want to buy it. They can also explain why their offer is the one that is most likely to close. Include anything that would help the seller feel confident that your deal will close on time.

Present in Person

In all multiple offers, try to present the offer in person. You're much more powerful when you're at the presentation. You can pick up on the sellers' frame of mind and build rapport with them.

You have the opportunity to speak with the sellers and may be able to assess the possible pain points of the sellers and modify offer to "ease their pain". You have an opportunity to make a positive impression on the sellers and make the case for your clients. It also means you have more of an opportunity to discuss possible options with the listing REALTOR®, such as closing date, condition date (if any), chattels, etc.

Make sure you have your clients on standby at a convenient location such as a local coffee shop or outside in their car. That way you can make any changes or sign off on counters immediately rather than waiting.

Service, Service, Service

Servicing the buyer doesn't end once you've shown them some homes and written and negotiated an offer. It's when your time to shine truly begins. Everything you've done to this point is just a foretaste of the kind of service you're going to provide that's really going to wow your clients.

As with everything, a systematized approach to the management of the purchase is a must. The Buyers' Task List details each step to be taken in making sure everything progresses as smoothly as possible.

Going, Going...

Your first task, should there be a financing condition, will be to make sure a copy of the purchase contract and supporting documentation is sent to your buyer's financial institution. However, simply assuming that they've received it and that they are aware of the condition dates involved can lead to many headaches. It's advisable to request that they confirm that they've received the information and then reconfirm the condition removal date and then document your conversation with them.

Staying on top of this condition is an absolute must if you're committed to outstanding service. It's never a good idea to leave the information with the financial institution and then wait to hear from them.

Several years ago, I had a transaction in which I had sent the purchase agreement and listing information to the mortgage broker the night it had been signed. I checked with him in the morning to confirm that he had received it. The condition date was seven days after acceptance, and as part of my buyers' system, I called him two days before the scheduled removal date. When I spoke with him, he had no idea what transaction I was talking about, so I reminded him of the client's name and the fact that the conditions had to be removed in two days. I could hear him shuffling paper on his desk. Suddenly he gasped and said he had just found the transaction. It turns out he had put it on his desk and had inadvertently piled other papers on top and forgotten about it. As a result, I had to go back to the sellers and get an additional two day extension; a pain, yes, but at least it avoided something which could have had much more serious consequences. Had I simply waited to hear from him, it's likely that the deal would have collapsed. Part of your system should be to have a quick check back with the financial institution at least two days prior to the condition removal date to help ensure things are progressing smoothly or to take any remedial action necessary.

The next component of your system is the management of the home inspection. If your offer contains a home inspection condition, your next conversation should be with the home inspector. You'll want to confirm the date and time of the inspection and coordinate this with your client.

You may consider calling the inspector when you write the offer and tentatively book a date and time while the clients are with you. You can then reconfirm with everyone once the offer has been accepted. This also has the advantage of being able to let the listing REALTOR® know that your buyers are serious and have already booked the date for the inspection, which may help in the negotiations.

When booking the inspection, it's a good idea to have scheduled it at least one day prior to the condition removal date. In the event that there are some issues that need to be resolved, it becomes incredibly stressful on the buyers, the sellers and both REALTORS® should any negotiations required have to be conducted at the last minute. I've had the experience of trying to negotiate having the sellers repair or replace items that were found on the inspection in the final hours before condition removal. Needless to say, it is challenging and stressful in the extreme and your clients won't thank you for putting them through it.

Managing the inspection will involve confirming the inspection with the listing REALTOR® and the inspector the day before it's scheduled. On the day of the inspection, you'll want to show up early so you can meet with the inspector and introduce them to the client. During the inspection, you'll find it helpful to follow the clients around. Be prepared to ask questions to clarify and help your clients understand what the inspector is pointing out to them as well as to help you grow in your knowledge of household systems. I fully believe that a great inspector will point out both the trivial and the serious to the clients, but will explain it in a way that the client understands the difference and helps them make as informed a decision as they can.

I once used an inspector who wasn't able to help the clients distinguish the difference between a deficiency and normal wear and tear; serious issues and those that simply required some spackle and paint. Most of the problems encountered were simple wear and tear items and were easily repaired with a minimum of expense to either party. Without having asked him to clarify how much each of the repairs would cost, the clients would have lost the home they loved and I would have lost the transaction. I never used that inspector again. It can be a challenge, as a new Sales Representative, to find this kind of inspector, but by asking your more experienced colleagues, you'll find it easier to determine the inspector with whom you'll feel comfortable.

One of the issues that crops up occasionally as part of the removal of the inspection condition is that of renegotiating the purchase price due to defects uncovered during the inspection. It's important to educate your buyer so that they understand that unless there are major problems, there is small likelihood of a major price reduction. Every home will have some flaws in it. Minor issues, such as holes in the walls, leaky faucets, light switches installed upside down and others of this nature are best dealt with by having the sellers repair them. However, when the issue becomes more serious, such as a furnace that needs replacing, or a serious crack in the basement wall, your client can expect to have some wiggle room to renegotiate the price. Your major task will be to help them understand that they can't expect to buy a home without any issues, and therefore they can't expect to either decrease the price by the total of the cost of repair or replacement of the problem item or to have the sellers pay for the total cost of replacement. They need to be prepared to accept that they may have to negotiate a deal where the seller and the buyer each pay for a portion of the cost.

When dealing with the condition regarding the Status Certificate or Condo Documents issues that crop up often are,

- when they have to be produced,

- how long they remain valid once ordered and

- trying to set a date for condition removal.

Depending upon the provincial legislation, condominium corporations have a specified time period to provide the documents. In Ontario, condo corporations have 10 days following a request and payment of the fees for the document to produce the documents.

When writing an offer with a clause regarding the Status Certificate, to ensure complete clarity, it is strongly advised it be worded to include a specific date for condition removal, which includes the 10 day waiting period. Should the listing REALTOR® obtain it earlier, you can always amend the date.

"This offer is conditional upon the Buyer's lawyer reviewing the Status Certificate and attachments and finding the Status Certificate and Attachments satisfactory in the Buyer's Lawyer's sole and absolute discretion. The (Buyer/Seller) _____ agrees to request at the (Buyer's/Seller's) _____ expense, the Status Certificate and attachments within _____ days of acceptance of this Offer. Unless the buyer gives notice in writing to the Seller personally or in accordance with any other provisions for the delivery of notice in this Agreement of Purchase and Sale or any Schedule thereto not later than 5 p.m. on _____, that this condition is fulfilled, this Offer shall be null and void and the deposit shall be returned to the Buyer in full without deduction. This condition is included for the benefit of the Buyer and may be waived at the Buyer's sole option by notice in writing to the Seller as aforesaid within the time period stated herein."

The uncontrollable and therefore most frustrating part of managing the Status Certificate condition is the wait for them to be delivered. Part of your management of this period will be to stay in contact with the listing REALTOR® to make sure you receive the documents as timely and as smoothly as possible and to keep your clients calm during the wait. As before, it's important to check with the client two days before the condition removal date to ensure things are on track.

Gone

Condition removal is a time of both relief and stress for the REALTOR® and the client. It can be extremely stressful if there are unexpected delays or should issues crop up at the last minute. That's why your Buyer Service System must ensure that you've stayed on top of all the conditions and been in communication with everyone involved in the transaction.

Notices, Waivers and Amendments

So the conditions are ready to be removed and the sale will be firmed up. One of the most common faux pas occurring at this point is the use of the incorrect form for condition removal. Many people are confused about when to use a Waiver, a Notice of Fulfillment and an Amendment. In order to better understand when to use these forms, it's necessary to understand what each form actually means.

A Waiver allows a party to a contract to proceed with the agreement without actually fulfilling the specific terms of the condition. This would occur in a situation where circumstances arise which are different from those envisioned when the conditions were drafted. In these instances, the condition has been met, but not in accordance with the exact terms expressed in the agreement.

For example, I want to buy a condo and include a condition of review of the status certificate as shown previously. However, I've worked as a property manager and understand how to review the status certificate and therefore don't need my lawyer to review them. When I'm ready to remove the condition, since I haven't actually fulfilled the terms of the condition by having my lawyer review the documents, I would have to use a Waiver.

A Notice of Fulfillment is used when the actual terms of the condition have been met, such as in the following instance. I have included a financing condition whereby my financing has to be met to my approval. Once the financial institution has provided the financing to my approval, I would then remove the condition using a Notice of Fulfillment.

The major issue that occurs is the use of an **Amendment** to remove the condition. Unless it is both parties' intention to actually remove the condition from the agreement, this form should **never** be used. This misstep most frequently occurs in cases in which a property inspection has revealed some problems with the home and both parties have either negotiated a price reduction or the seller has agreed to complete some work required to repair the issues. In these cases, the issue arises where an Amendment has been used to delete the condition of inspection and also insert a clause stating that the sellers will complete the work required or that the price has been adjusted. This is the **wrong** use of the form.

The correct method of handling this issue would be to use this form to **amend the contract** by inserting the clause regarding the work required or the price adjustment and have the buyer sign the form. They would also sign a Waiver since the condition is being fulfilled, but not to their satisfaction since the inspection revealed concerns. The Amendment would then be sent to the sellers for signature and once it has been received back from the seller, the Waiver would then be transmitted. In this way, the contract is modified only to include the new terms and the condition is waived.

Since this chapter is not meant as a comprehensive guide on forms, but merely as a review of the most common conditions, it's your responsibility and in your best interest, any time you have a question about which form to use and when, that you consult your Broker or Manager.

Business Building Exercise

Here's another business building exercise, and one I think is critical to your long term success. **Find a number of available listings of all different kinds (single family, condo, multifamily, properties with tenants, etc.) and write offers for each of them. Use different conditions and terms to make them as real as possible and have your broker or manager check them to make sure they're accurate and realistic.**

After the Sold Sign Goes Up

Now that you've removed conditions and the deal is firm, there are a number of things you can do to reinforce yourself as the REALTOR® to whom your clients will want to refer their friends and family. This is where your Buyer's Task List and Deal Tracking Form will help guide you through the paperwork jungle. Your post-sale service system will need to ensure that your clients are kept informed of the next steps they'll need to take on the way towards closing the sale, including preparing for the move, ensuring they've spoken with their lawyer and any additional inspections have been scheduled. Your main task through this period will be to act as a point of reference or guide to ensure they understand each step and that things are able to progress smoothly.

It's always handy to be able to provide the buyers with a moving guide so they're aware of what steps to take to ensure their move proceeds smoothly. I've included the one I put together from various companies, but you may want to consider using the one that your moving company uses.

On closing day, I ask my buyers to let me know when they plan on being at the new house. That way I can do a walkthrough with them to ensure that the property is in the shape they expected and to deal with any issues which may have occurred. After all, you want to know the problems so that you can deal with them. That's how you can provide the stellar customer service your clients expect and become known as the REALTOR® that goes the extra mile for their clients.

One of the many questions I get is what to get the buyers when they take possession of their new home. There are many different options, including gift cards, but one of the best that I've heard is to provide them with a catered lunch on moving day. That could be as simple as bringing in sub sandwiches and drinks, a box of fried chicken with sides or anything else that they don't have to prepare. I've heard of an agent who stocks their clients' fridges with essentials like milk, bread, eggs, butter, veggies and fruit. While going to the store and picking up the groceries and then delivering them for each client could be a big time commitment, some of the large grocery chains now offer delivery options that make organizing something like that simple, time- and cost-effective.

However, it's not just the closing gift you give them that will make you stand out in their minds and keep you in their thoughts when they meet someone who's thinking about buying or selling. It's your after sale service system that solidifies you as a "rock star".

The 1, 1, 1 System

Your system should include a method of staying in touch with the client once the sale has closed and they've moved into their new home. You'll want to make sure you speak to them:

• On the day after they've moved in, to find out if everything has gone smoothly and if there are any issues that may have cropped up overnight, so you can deal with them.

• One week later to ensure things are still going smoothly and to answer any questions they may have about the property or the neighbourhood.

• One month later to reconfirm that there are no issues and to let them know that should they have any need for service people or contractors that you have access to a wide range of providers.

At this point you'll need to transfer them from your active clients list to your database and set them up on your Referral Management System.

Business Building Exercise

Set up your post-sale Buyer's Service System.

THE BUYERS' SYSTEM

WHAT'S UP NEXT?

VOLUME 5 – I'M JUST SAYIN'

THE ART OF COMMUNICATION

"Wise Men speak because they have something to say. Fools, because they have to say something" - **Plato**

One of the single most important skills we need to have, as REALTORS®, is the ability to communicate clearly and effectively with our clients, colleagues and support people. This, though, goes far beyond the simple exchange of words. Communication is much more than just the transfer of information from one person to another. Effective communication is composed not only of the information itself, but also takes into account the medium through which the transfer of the information occurs, such as books, magazines and letters, electronic media, including radio, TV, email, and "simple" conversation. As well, the purpose behind the transfer, the non-verbal communication between the parties, including body language and gestures, how we dress or act and the ability of the person on the other end of the transfer to clearly hear and understand the information will all affect the effectiveness of that transfer.

Here's what you can expect in Volume 5 – I'm Just Sayin'

- The Art of Communication
- Communication Styles
- Get the message out

WHAT'S UP NEXT?

- Listen, Ask, Listen Again
- Key Principles of Active Listening
- Objection Handling
  - I'm Not Ready Yet!
  - Where do they come from?
  - Early and Often
  - The BASIQs
  - Go for the Close
  - Listen, Ask and Listen Again
  - The Specifics, including:
    - Sellers' Objections
    - Buyers' Objections
- Negotiation 101
  - Successful Negotiating = Good Planning
  - Define the Context
  - Define the Outcome
  - Set the Gameplan
  - Let the Negotiations Commence
  - Focus on Interests not Positions
  - Separate People from Problems
  - Provide Options for Mutual Gain
  - Use Objective Criteria not Emotion

- Establish your Bottom Line
- It's about getting what they want
- Make the Other Side Look Good
- Time equals Money
- Participation
- Negotiation Pointers
- Case Studies
- Advertising: Get the word out
  - Why should you market yourself?
  - Identify & Define your Brand
  - Establish a Marketing Strategy
  - Establish Your Marketing Budget
  - Advertising
  - Preparation
  - Creativity
  - Target the Right People
  - Knowledge of the Property
  - Structure of the Ad

WHAT'S UP NEXT?

SUMMARY

In the previous volume, we discussed how to manage listings. As a new Sales Representative, it's often easier to find and work with buyers. However, the principles of making presentations that focus on providing value to prospective clients, based on what the prospect is looking for, rather than on what you believe your value is remains the same as it does for listings.

Of significant importance, when working with buyers, is the necessity of qualifying them for motivation and the ability to purchase properties. You'll need to ask loads of open ended questions to get them to open up in order for you to find out just how motivated they are. In a later volume, we'll discuss the skill of actually closing for the offer.

Once you have the buyers committed and you've found them a home, your major task will be to shepherd them through the purchase process. This will require that you have a comprehensive system to follow which will ensure that everything runs smoothly and that you provide the outstanding service you promised to the client. Just as for a listing, that service will depend on having a system in place that allows you to perform a consistent sequence of tasks for each and every buyer. A sequence which must include the processes that will ensure that the offer is written correctly, conditions are managed in such a way as to reduce the potential for issues to arise and are removed within the timeframes required by the offer in which it should, and routines to ensure that you are able to prospect the listing so as to get more listings and buyers.

On the Right Foot

And now, your task will be to complete the Business Building Exercises in the Workbook; developing your Informed Buyer's Guide, Buyer's Presentation, and your Buyer's Management systems. You'll need to spend a significant amount of time role-playing your presentation, objection handling skills and your closing skills, but by investing the time now, you'll save yourself significant missteps and be that much closer to getting your career started off on the right foot. Good luck!

FOUNDATIONS FOR SUCCESS SERIES

Volume 1 - "On the Right Foot"
Business Planning, Organization and Real
Estate Etiquette

Volume 2 - "Good Hunting"
Prospecting and Lead Follow Up,

Volume 3 - "Listings, Listings, Listings"
Listings and Listing Systems,

Volume 4 - "Buyers, Buyers, Buyers",
Buyers and Buyers Systems

Volume 5 - "I'm Just Sayin"
Objection Handling, Communication and
Negotiation and Advertising

Volume 6 – The Workbook
Specific Business Building Exercises

Volume 7 – The Complete Series
All the volumes in one book, including the
Workbook.

Purchase individual volumes or the complete series
through the website at
www.foundationsforsuccess.ca

Steve began his real estate career in Edmonton, Alberta in 2001. He worked as an Associate Broker with Realty Executives North Star until 2008 when he opened his own brokerage. He moved back to Toronto in 2010, has been the Director of Agent Development for HomeLife/Cimerman Real Estate Ltd., Director of Training and Development for RE/MAX West Realty Inc., and Manager and Coach for The Daryl King Team at Royal LePage Your Community Realty and has designed and overseen the training, development and coaching of the sales personnel at each. He is the author of ''List to Last - The Definitive Guide to Finding, Closing and Managing Residential Listings''.

FOUNDATIONS FOR SUCCESS